Girl, You're a Grown Ass Woman

ROBIN HACKETT

DEDICATION

To all of my amazing Grown Ass Women friends,
Veronica, Debbie M, Angie, Alva, Gayle, Deb J, Diane, Lori B, Perri, Cecilia,
Lahoma, Colleen, Tina
Most importantly, this book is dedicated to all of **my music students** who made me very
aware of the person I was becoming!
And so many more who have influenced who I am today! *A Grown Ass Woman!*

ACKNOWLEDGMENTS

I would like to acknowledge my mother Carol Hackett who keeps me on course, Tracy Brown, Center for Spiritual Living Dallas, Petra Weldes Lisa Ferraro, Erika Luckett, Branice McKenzie Cynthia Landrum, Oshunfemi and all of my ancestors before me.
To my honorary Grown Ass Women, Gary Floyd, Glenn Morshower, and Andy Herzman
You guys rock my world!

TABLE OF CONTENTS

GIRL, YOU'RE A GROWN ASS WOMAN

FOREWARD

In August of 2012, I found myself in a number of conversations with women in their 40's and 50's who were out dating, and they would call me up and express their angst over not knowing what a love interest was thinking, why hadn't the person called, receiving mixed messages, etc. Surprisingly enough to me, my response was "Girl, You're a Grown Ass Woman, why don't you ask the person directly instead of guessing?"

Then the following Sunday at my church, I overheard a conversation between two women in their 30's and I heard one of them say, "Well, I can't tell if we really have a connection or if I am imagining an attraction." I popped my head into the conversation and said, "Girl, You're a Grown Ass Woman, why don't you ask and then you won't have to guess."

Here were examples of three different generations of women having the same conversation surrounding love interests. Through the years I have often seen women, including myself, wait by the telephone wondering why a certain person had not called, or when they did call, hang onto every word and tuck it away somewhere to share with girlfriends later, so we could figure out together what they meant by this and by that. Ya'll know this is a form of insanity.

had been aware of this in myself for years, but wasn't sure how it could be different. But when those words came out of my mouth, "Girl, You're a Grown Ass Woman," it felt empowering. I began saying it more and more. I talked with female friends of mine and we all began to discover there were some key places in our lives where we were not acting like Grown Ass Women, but like shrinking wallflowers.

Like it or not, we women are still indoctrinated with mixed and conflicting messages about what it is to be a woman. Sit and watch an afternoon of television and be aware of the commercials or spend a day watching Lifetime Television for Women.

Scan the covers of women's magazines. It is as if we must be equipped with dueling personalities. Many TV shows and commercials show women being powerful and strong and then in the same instance, we are whitening our teeth, coloring our hair, wearing the right makeup, getting thin...........all so we can attract the right partner or be the *right* person. Mixed messages, ya think?

I was inspired to send an email to some of my female friends entitled, "Grown Ass Women United," with guidelines on how a Grown Ass Woman walks through the world. The more we talked about it, the more places we saw where we could improve and begin to act like Grown Ass Women.

This book is about those places where we could walk, talk, and be different in the world. It is intended for all women, young and old, gay and straight, black, white, red, yellow and brown.

I was drawn to writing this book. It is my own quest to live powerfully in all aspects of my life. I hope it inspires you to do the same.

INTRODUCTION

At the end of each chapter is a section called **Just for You**. You will find pertinent questions and exercises that pertain to each chapter's subject matter. Please know that these exercises are not the end all be all, but are there to point you in the direction of becoming a Grown Ass Woman.

Once you begin the journey, there will be many amazing, synchronistic "coincidences" and events that will appear for you that will reveal more and more what it is to be a Grown Ass Woman.

Take your time through the exercises. No need to be in a hurry. Remember, you are in the process of changing your life. No small matter. In some instances, there may not be enough empty pages provided, so you may want to purchase a special journal for your Grown Ass Woman thoughts and exercises.

Perhaps you can share this process with a friend. Since starting this book and the Facebook page , I now feel so connected to other women. We are truly a sisterhood and I love how amazing each and every one of us is. Enjoy your process and don't forget to celebrate yourself all the time!

Blessings!

CHAPTER 1

A GROWN-ASS WOMAN KNOWS HER WORTH

After my last relationship ended, someone suggested that I write down 50-100 qualities I would want in a partner. I loved this suggestion at the time but I have now discovered I need to recognize 50 amazing qualities about myself. And believe it or not, many women are not taught about self-worth and about focusing on their own amazing qualities.

I have been teaching for nine years and I have watched some of my bold and fierce little girls turn into fumbling, insecure teenagers mostly concerned with how they look and appear to others. I was shocked to watch some girls dropping their interests to become consumed with boys, clothes, and makeup. I get it. However, we need to balance this passage with other strong and powerful messages for them.

We tend to look outward toward others for our worth when indeed, it is best that we look inward first in order for our outward to change. If we do not know our value alone, we cannot stand together with anyone, partner or otherwise. When we do not know our worth, we become a burden on the world, dragging every situation that we are involved in downward. You must begin to know where you stand alone before you stand solidly in relationship. And everything in life is relationship.

What does it mean to know our worth? To me it means to really recognize those qualities within myself that I love. It is also to be my own best friend, my own cheerleader, and my own coach.

I have spent a good majority of my life looking at what's wrong with me as opposed to what's right with me. What a way to live. It is not a powerful place to live from. It weighs down your entire being to live this way, both energetically and physically.

When you know your own worth, value and purpose in life you walk, talk, and act in a very different way than when you don't know. We have all seen those women who seem to just get that. They do indeed make an impression wherever they go.

Many of us came from homes where we did not gain our own sense of self-worth. We did not experience what it was to feel safe in the world. If you do not feel safe in the world, then you tend to not trust people, situations, and most of all, you don't trust yourself.

If you came from a home that did not make you feel safe and did not cheer you on, then you must begin to do that for yourself. So we are going to look forward. Let's start with, ***everyday is a new day.*** Begin where you are and move forward into expansion of what is possible for you.

If you are not living your life right now as a Grown Ass Woman, it is because you are living from a place of contraction, not expansion. Start now to name and claim your worth. Take a stand for yourself.

My philosophy is this, it is none of my business what people say of me or think of me. I am what I am and I do what I do. I expect nothing and accept everything. And it makes life so much easier.

Anthony Hopkins
Actor

This statement is important to take in. How many times during your day do you wonder what others are thinking of you? Am I up to par? Am I pretty enough? Am I smart enough? Do they like me? Did I do something to offend them? UGH! No more!

We have all heard the saying, "What you think of me is none of my business." This statement is not being arrogant or rude. It is the truth. What do YOU think of you? What do YOU want? Do YOU like yourself?

So many people are angry at their parents for their childhood, indulging in victim behavior. They are angry no one nurtured them or their talents the way they wanted. Well the reality is, your parents did the best they knew how, not the best that they could, but the best they knew how. So now it's up to you to grow yourself up.

There is no one outside of you that can give you your self-worth. No job can do it, no amount of money can do it, and the richest, best looking partner cannot do it. Only YOU can do this for YOU!

We have all at one time or another looked outside of ourselves for affirmation. In my case, I finally realized that no matter how many times people told me that I was an amazing singer, I would still wait to hear those words after every performance.

I believed that if I wasn't a famous singer, admired by all, making lots of money and getting Grammy Awards, that I must not be that good. What I was really seeking was for *everyone* to love my music and if they loved my music on this global level, it meant that I was finally somebody in this world and that I was loveable as well.

Well, I am not world famous, but I have had some level of "success." Nonetheless, I would hear people compliment me when I would perform and I would still negate my music and my voice and see myself as not good enough. I have heard many world famous people interviewed and they have the same "I'm not good enough" thing going on. We can never feel fully worthy if we think our worth comes from what people are thinking and saying about us. Because one day they like you, and the next day they may not.

So let's go exploring. This self-worth thing is not to be taken lightly. You're going to have to work on it each and every day. It's worth it though.

JUST FOR YOU!

For thirty days, make an appointment with yourself to spend time with you. A woman, who knows her worth, loves spending time with herself and feels good about spending time with herself. Put it on your calendar as an actual appointment and do not let anything get in the way of that appointment and you. One way to build self-esteem and worth is to be your word. Do what you say you are going to do. Every time you do what you say you are going to do, you are building self-esteem and worth. You will feel better about yourself and who you are for following through. When you follow through, the gift you get is for you!

Write down 50 qualities about YOU that YOU love! Anything that you love about you!

Example:

I love that I have big beautiful eyes.

I love how funny I am.

I love that I multi-task really well.

Read these qualities out loud everyday for 30 days! Write about how you feel when you say these qualities out loud.

Take one or two of these qualities and stand in front of a mirror. Look in your eyes, and say the qualities as affirmations to yourself. Repeat these affirmations as many times as you can remember during the day. Write about your experience. How you do you feel? Is there resistance?

Take up an activity that you have always thought about doing. Have no goal in mind. Do it for the sake of doing it. Do not measure yourself and let it have nothing to do with a natural talent you have. Try something new. Have fun!

Write down some ideas and thoughts about this! Remember, you are not trying to achieve anything here. Write down what you think the purpose of this exercise is.

Example: Take roller skating lessons, learn to garden, write poetry, take cooking classes, learn to knit, etc....

Write down this phrase and finish it as many times as is necessary, then say each phrase out loud.

I release my need to play small............. (Ex., in my career), because I am a Grown Ass Woman, capable, strong, and worthy!

How does it feel to say these phrases out loud? Use this phrase as often as possible to remind yourself who you are!

STOP! Stop speaking negatively or poorly about yourself. When you begin to say something negative about yourself, turn it around or plug in one of the qualities you wrote down. You wouldn't allow your friends to say negative things about themselves, so don't allow yourself to do so either. Ya'll know that's a form of insanity. Just crazy. Think about it.

I can actually say I have practiced these exercises and they work. All we are doing is re-patterning old funky, negative thoughts into new thoughts about ourselves that are more positive and powerful. Yes, it will take some work, but aren't YOU worth it?

This is what I discovered: If I am going to live on this earth, I might as well live powerfully and positively instead of fearfully and negatively. Decide you are going to enjoy your life and love who you are, no matter what. Make that decision for yourself, by discovering and knowing your worth. No excuses! Why?

Girl, You're a Grown Ass Woman:, capable, strong, and worthy!

CHAPTER 2

A GROWN-ASS WOMAN KNOWS WHAT SHE HAS TO OFFER

I went over and over in my mind what the difference was between a woman knowing her worth, and a woman knowing what she has to offer. After having numerous conversations with some of my Grown Ass Women friends, it was concluded that knowing your worth comes from the inside. It is what you intrinsically know and love about yourself and who you are. Knowing what you have to offer has to do with the gifts and actions that you give to the world, whether globally, in your community, or in your family.

When I was a little girl, I would get lost playing the piano or playing my guitar for hours and hours. The same was true for me with writing and acting. I loved to write short plays and stories. Then, I would gather all my friends in the neighborhood and make them act out the play or sing whatever songs I wrote. To this day, I can still get lost in those activities. I have been a professional singer and songwriter for most of my life and I am still organizing people to come together and create.

About nine years-ago I started writing a book (not this one), something I never thought of doing, but one day I started writing and found myself lost in it for hours, just as I did as a little girl. This is a clue as to what I have to offer. I am passionate about it. I do it *just because.* I get lost in it. I do it because it is fun and brings me joy.

I lived in New York City for over 20 years trying to make a go of it as a singer/songwriter. I spent so many of those years seeking fame and fortune, so much so, that I lost the joy of just playing and writing. I eventually left New York City and moved to Texas where I "coincidentally" fell into teaching private voice lessons, piano, and guitar to children.

I also began teaching acting and musical theater at a Children's Community Theater. I did not realize that I would find so much joy from teaching children and I realized this was a gift that I had. This was part of what I had to offer in the world. I created workshops for the children as well and eventually became the Artistic Director of that theater. I created programs for children as well as adults. It is all part of what I had been doing as a little girl.

When you know what you have to offer you feel your value in the world. You feel good and alive and on purpose in your life. It is an exhilarating feeling and you feel good about yourself. So, what is that for you? Have you honed in on it? Are you doing it?

Please understand, I am not asking about your job in the world currently. I am asking what your gifts are. What is it that you are inherently inclined towards? It is usually something you get lost in, something you cannot imagine life without, something you are passionate about, and lastly it brings you joy and fulfillment.

Some folks do have jobs that are connected with their gifts, but what I am talking about is discovering and defining your gifts. I am not talking about you being the next Mother Teresa or Oprah! Just wanting you to become aware of what you are good at.

My mother is very crafty. She is in heaven when she is sewing, and cross-stitching, and creating arts and crafts of any kind. She has been doing this since I was a little girl. She has always seemed so quietly content and n joy when she is creating in this way. She does not sell these items. She nakes them for her own joy and for her home and family.

What is it for you? Teacher, mother, counselor, inventor, doctor, scrap-booker, quilter, organizer, lover of children, saving animals, alternative healer, cook, gardener......

JUST FOR YOU

Write down activities you would get lost in as a child?

Can you write about what you are passionate about? What gets you excited and on fire? Where do you shine in the world?

What do your friends say you have to offer the world? Call your friends and ask them what they notice you are good at?

Once you discover what you have to offer, are you offering these gifts in the world? If you are not, spend some time journaling about why. What comes up for you?

List ways you can offer these gifts to your family, community, the world!

Write down five steps you can take in the next few days toward giving what you have to offer to the world.

Why do we want to know what we offer? It is simply because it allows us another reason to feel good about ourselves and to esteem ourselves. In regards to our relationships, we are certainly much more interesting and enjoyable to be around when we feel good about ourselves in the world.

When you know your worth and are clear about what you have to offer, you become a light in the world, a helper, a giver. You become someone everyone wants to be around. Many of us are still functioning in the world seeking approval, wondering what value we have. Everyone has value! Name it, Claim it, Be it! Why?

Girl, You're a Grown Ass Woman:, capable, strong, and worthy!

CHAPTER 3

A GROWN ASS WOMAN TRUSTS AND LISTENS TO HERSELF

Nobody ever taught me when I was young how to make decisions. So throughout my life I have used hunches and my own intuition. I have made some bold moves in my life that other people thought were crazy. But I have never regretted those choices and the biggest, boldest moves I have made have always turned out well.

I equate this intuition or instinct to "a still small voice" that pops into my mind at a split second and sets me into immediate action and motion or alert.

For me, it can cause excitement and a feeling of forward motion, or an uncomfortable feeling in my body. On the other hand, there have been times that the still small voice or hunch whispered to me and I ignored it. Some were just mundane events and other times it had to do with entering into a situation where the voice said, "No, that's not a good idea, and a big red flag went up".

I would feel a discomfort in my body. I have ignored this voice at times because I wanted whatever it was so badly, I was not centered enough in myself to make a decision based on anything else but the need to fill a hole in myself. These situations included business deals and relationships with men. They always turned out disastrous and crazy.

I was once getting ready to perform on a TV show, and the night before one of my band members who lived nearby asked me if I wanted him to drive his car and I hesitated answering him. In that moment, a thought came across my mind that my car might not work properly. I had no logical reason to believe that it was not working properly, just a feeling. So I said no, let's take my car.

The next morning he drove to my place in his car. He asked me if I wanted him to drive and I hesitated once again because that feeling came across that my car might not work. But I replied that we could drive my car. Needless to say, we drove my car and on the way to the show in the middle of rush hour traffic, we got a flat tire. I didn't trust my intuition or listen to that feeling!

I was brought up during a time when what I saw on TV were women who were dependent on their husbands, playing small and weak, seeking their approval, seeking their protection, and their love. Carol Brady, June Cleaver, Laura Petrie, Donna Reed etc... I loved all of these shows, but the man was always in charge and always knew better.

So during the time I worked in the corporate world, I was surrounded by older men in management who "appeared" to have it all together and "appeared" to be in the know. They were men who inevitably would have one too many drinks at the yearly Christmas party and say something inappropriate or "accidentally" grab where they shouldn't have. I knew it was ugly and wrong but I was too afraid to complain.

I was always afraid if I made a complaint, I would be hushed. I was afraid I would be ostracized and no one would like me. Wow! It is disturbing to me that I once lived this way.

I have made boyfriends the end all be all and I always thought they knew better. Of course this put a lot of pressure on them and on the relationship. I have stayed in friendships and relationships where I felt disrespected and dishonored, all because I didn't want to be by myself or trust that there could be anything or anyone better for me. I assure you, there was always a voice telling me to go and I would stay on, thinking things would change or they didn't really mean to be the way they were.

I would stay to try and win them over. Win them over? As if they were the prize I had to have. We don't have to win anybody over, we don't have to settle for poor behavior, and we have the right to speak up for ourselves. When we know our worth and know what we have to offer, we can trust and listen to our own intuition. We don't have to be afraid to leave a situation, job, or partner. We feel safe in the world because our foundation is based on our own worth and our own intuition. We know we deserve different.

Listen to that big red flag that is accompanied by bells and whistles. Trust your hunches and intuition. If you are not sure what that is because you are not used to it, then take your time when making decisions regarding any part of your life. Listen to those uncomfortable feelings in your body. It's giving you a heads up that something is off. Gather all the data you can before making a decision.

Be willing to make a decision and if it is the wrong decision, know you can trust yourself to re-adjust that decision and create something else.

You can change your mind anytime. Practice taking your time. I have noticed there is a feeling that I get when I've made a decision that feels right. There is calm in my body, my mind, and my emotions. Everything feels settled and in alignment. The more you begin to know your worth and what you have to offer the more you will honor yourself and be willing to take the time and space to listen for your inner voice. You have nothing to lose but a little time.

A Grown Ass Woman listens and trusts herself, but she also listens intently and carefully to what others are saying when she enters situations. People tell you who they are right up front. I was once entering into a business arrangement and the other person told me that all the other business partners she had in the past had all left abruptly and that all those partnerships ended in a horrible fight. There is a reason she told me this. It was true. Don't pretend that you will be the one business partner they have that it won't end in disaster. Listen.

If you meet a potential love interest and they say they will never marry, listen. They mean it, so don't believe you are going to be the one to change the person. Listen to yourself and listen for what others are saying about themselves. Trust yourself to make choices that honor, support, and respect who you want to be in the world. Practice not asking for anyone's advice just for a period of time. You must get used to being your own "center," your own inner guidance. Please know this is just a practice. A GAW also knows when and how to ask for advice on a subject she is not that well versed in. But here, I am talking more about finding and making friends with your inner compass and not seeking information.

JUST FOR YOU!

Write about a situation(s) where you did not listen to yourself or trust yourself.

Recall and write about a situation(s) where you did listen to your intuition and trusted yourself.

What was the difference in feeling, emotion, and mentality between the situations you identified in both questions above?

Identify a situation that you need to make a decision on, no matter how big or small. Write about what it would be like to say yes to the situation. All the possibilities and all the consequences, good and bad. Then write about what it would be like to say no with all the possibilities and consequences. Notice how you feel when you are writing both scenarios. Notice how you feel physically, and mentally, and notice what emotions come up. Write it all down!

Write a vision statement about how you would like to be treated in the world and about the kind of person you would like to be in your relationships and within your work environment.

When someone asks you to do something, tell them you will get back to them. Don't say yes right away. Give yourself time. This is a fun practice to do for just the mundane things in life. Write about what it feels like to not answer right away!

Use the above exercises as tools to practice listening for what is true and right for you. You will begin to respond to life as opposed to react to life and life decisions. This is when true listening and trusting one's self begins to take hold. No one knows what is best for you more than you, and no one can make decisions about your life, your partner, your career, your anything, better than you. Why?

Girl, You're A Grown Ass Woman:, capable, strong, and worthy!

CHAPTER 4

A GROWN ASS WOMAN TREATS HERSELF WELL

When I was a younger woman living in New York and struggling to make a life, I would talk to my parents once a week on Sunday and I would occasionally complain and feel depressed that all wasn't going my way.

My mom would ask me when was the last time I bought something for myself or did something to make myself feel good. She said that it was important to do something to make you feel good even if it was purchasing something small like a nice bar of French soap that might cost $10 or a pedicure.

I have always remembered that phone conversation. There have been times when I could not even swing a little something so instead I would go for a walk or sit outside and watch the sunrise or sunset. Anything that makes me feel good. Anything that could shift my energy.

I speak on this because many times we expect our friends or our partner to make us feel good or to treat us well. But if we are already doing this for ourselves, whatever someone else does is just icing on the cake. Taking care of ourselves leaves us powerful in the world and not needy.

Do not be needy in your relationships. You can have needs but do not be needy. Know how to take care of yourself because you love how you feel when you do it. So let's get down to it. This is a big one for all of us women!

If you don't like the way your body looks, then do what you need to do to feel good about your body. Do this only to please you, not anyone else. Hear this again. If you don't like the way your body looks, then do what you need to do to feel good about your body. Do this only to please you, not anyone else.

Love being in your body because you like the way you look and feel. We are not victims here and we are not powerless to take control of how we look. It is empowering to love our bodies. There a millions of women in the world who are losing weight and taking care of their bodies. Are you uniquely defective in this area? Is it not possible for you? Don't believe that for a minute.

Think enough of yourself to take care of your body and take care of your body because you think enough of yourself.

You will feel powerful in your body if you love the way you feel in it. If you are overweight and unhealthy then only YOU can change that. No if s, ands, or buts about it. Currently, I am at a weight that does not make me feel empowered but for the last month and a half I have been taking actions to change that and I am feeling better already.

I have chosen to add some healthy items to my day. I make sure I have a salad everyday and I have fresh juice for one meal. It has changed how I feel about myself as well as caused me to lose excess pounds that no longer serve me.

Take actions to feel good about your food choices but not about losing weight. It's a subtle trick and it works. Treat yourself well. If you are overweight and you genuinely feel good about yourself then there is nothing to change unless you are unhealthy. I do know women friends who are overweight and look and feel beautiful and sexy. So I am not a believer that we all should be *skinny minis*. I am a believer that we all should feel good about ourselves and our bodies. That's it.

Wear what makes you feel good. Yes, it makes a difference. For me, I like matching underwear sets because I feel beautiful. At this point, nobody else sees them but I just like the way I feel. Do things like this for yourself whether you are in a relationship or not.

Purchase clothes that make you feel beautiful and unencumbered, no matter what your size; show your curves ...... for you. Love feeling feminine and sexy for nobody....but you.

I also love smelling good so I adhere to the 3- layer plan. Bath gel, lotion, and perfume of the same scent. Yummy. Love it. Make rituals around getting dressed and showering and bathing.

Do it even if no else experiences it but you. When I perform on stage, I like to wear perfume. Now, no one is on stage with me to smell it but it is just something that makes me feel good about myself.

Are your surroundings beautiful? How do you feel in your bedroom, living room, and kitchen? Are you living like a Grown Ass Woman or a college student? When I lived in New York, I still lived like a college student with a futon bed that I opened every night for bed and then closed it up for daytime.

Then I moved to Texas and it was exciting to purchase a real couch and not a futon. Sounds crazy huh! But a Grown Ass Woman has a home with grown up furniture in it. She has made a home for herself, a foundation that is also her woman cave that she can go back into and regenerate. Yes, I said woman cave because we need one too, and nine times out of ten it is our home.

Have rituals that don't involve anyone else. A Friday night bath with wine, a manicure/pedicure every Saturday. Take yourself to the movies without anyone else. Re-do your bathroom. Buy wonderful linens and bedspreads for your bedroom. Buy candles, perfume, soap, meditate, exercise, eat well, etc.....I am getting exciting just writing about it!

Clothing, underwear, soap, and perfume may all seem frivolous, but we are building a foundation that makes us feel solid inside our own skin, inside this new life we are creating. These chapters are all building a foundation of LOVE for yourself, for a greater YOU!
have a friend and every year in January she goes to the doctor and has
physical. In addition, she goes to her gynecologist. This has been

routine for her for years. I cannot say I have done that, but I am going to be a Grown Ass Woman and start doing it. Many of us have fears around the health of our bodies for different reasons.

I am a full-time artist, performer, and writer and up until now have had health insurance on and off. I am not saying you must have health insurance but I am saying you should have some way that you are taking care of your physical body, either through traditional medicine, alternative medicine, nutrition, or a combination of all......whatever it is for you.

Do it! As we all know if we do not have our health it is difficult to function in the world.

Every time I go to the doctor, I feel really good about having taken that action. When I don't go, it is because of imagined fears of something being wrong. We cannot afford to do that to ourselves. A Grown Ass Woman knows she can handle whatever life deals out.

Move your body! That's right. Whatever age you are, move your body. Walk, run, go to the gym, do yoga, stretch. Find what works for you and do it. This is part of treating yourself well!

Now that we've talked about how wonderful it is to treat yourself well, remember to keep treating yourself well no matter who is in your life and do not change your rituals for anyone, especially not a date.

When you meet a love interest, no matter what, stick with your rituals. If you have established a ritual on Friday night after work, arrange your date time before or after you've done that ritual. Do not neglect your rituals. Stick with it during the dating phase. Later you can decide if you want to make compromises within an established committed relationship.

So many women will throw out what has been established in order to have a date. They will cancel plans with friends if a potential love interest calls for a date. They act as if it will be their last date. Honor yourself by honoring your commitments to you as well as your friends and family members.

It is a gift to you to do good things for yourself that make you feel good. You deserve to feel good as much as possible. Do not neglect yourself! Treat yourself well. Why?

Girl, You're a Grown Ass Woman:, capable, strong, and worthy!

JUST FOR YOU!

Make a list of ways you can begin to treat yourself well.

Make a list of rituals you can start doing now that you've always wanted to do!

Identify 2 rituals that you can start this week and do them. Write about when you would do them, and commit to that time. Write about how you might feel when you do them.

Take yourself out on a date and buy something for yourself each time you get paid. Make it something small and under $15.

If you have not gone to a doctor in awhile for a routine check-up, write about why? Any fears? No insurance? Just haven't gone?

CHAPTER 5

A GROWN ASS WOMAN WALKS THROUGH HER FEARS

If you have a life dream but you are afraid to move toward it, too bad. **Get on it.** My friend Diane reminds me of this all the time. On the other side of your fear is exactly what you want waiting there for you. A Grown Ass Woman walks through her fears. She knows there is a gift on the other side. When we don't walk through our fears, we are acting as a child or teenager might act. But you're a Grown Ass Woman, so when you state that to yourself each and every day, it will give you the strength to move toward whatever you are afraid of.

The Nike commercial says, "Just Do It". Yeah, that is what it comes down to. I have friends who have been dreaming about their dream for 10 o 15 years and still have not taken any steps in the direction of their dream. We tip-toe around it. Many of us let other things get in the way of our dream or we listen to other people tell us how it is impossible or it will ever happen. But we won't know, until we try. We let fear run the show.

To go toward your dream, I admit can be scary. What if it doesn't work out? Well, what if it doesn't work out? .... Better yet, what if it does work out? Hey what a concept! Why not come out of the block with the notion that your dream could come true with some positive thought, persistence, and continuous action. A Grown Ass Woman knows she is powerful, and she believes there is nothing she cannot achieve with her belief in herself.

Because of the emerging of this in my life, I have felt for the first time that my dreams are coming true. I really believe in me and my talents and my power to create. I feel I won't fall off the wagon and give up on myself. I have let negative thoughts and beliefs keep me from my dream for many years.

It is important that you take responsibility for what is not happening in your life. If you look around at your life right now and you don't like what you see, how powerful is it to know that you had some choice in creating it. Now, you have a choice in how you want your life to look from here on out.

Grown Ass Women have confidence, remain persistent, and have a belief that they cannot fail. This is the first time in my life that I have felt all of these qualities. All because I discovered that I am a Grown Ass Woman. Wow! What a feeling! I have become a *yes woman*. Meaning, I have decided to say yes to any and all opportunities offered to me which are in alignment with my dream, no matter how scary.

In the past, I would not have been so open to say *yes* and I would subtly sabotage myself. A Grown Ass Woman knows that not everyone will like her or like what she does, but she moves forward anyway. A Grown Ass Woman has passion and confidence in what she has to offer, so she just offers it without reservation.

A Grown Ass Woman sets her intentions and then creates an environment for those intentions to unfold. She does not leave herself a way out or fool herself with excuses that cause her not to move forward. A Grown Ass Woman is teachable and willing to get advice about how she can move her dream forward. She is strong enough in who she is that she knows she doesn't know everything and therefore can listen to others' advice without it taking anything away from her personhood.

When a Grown Ass Woman goes after her dream and achieves it, she knows she is giving other women permission and incentive to make their dreams come true and this is part of the reason she goes after her dream.

She also knows when she achieves her dream she can be of even more value in the world because she has more resources and experience to do good in the world.

Sometimes a dream looks like it happened overnight when we are observing other people's dream. But it is never overnight. It is a conscious ongoing belief that your dream is on its way all the time. We must be persistent and consistent in thought and action. I will say it again. We must be persistent and consistent in thought and action.

I have started and stopped so many times in my life because someone said no to me.

This type of behavior will get you nowhere. Trust me, I know. But since becoming aware of my GAWness, I am at my desk everyday doing something toward my dream. I get up and shower and get dressed and I am at my desk by 9 am or 9:30am at the latest.

If you have a dream, you must realize that you are the CEO and CFO of your company (your dream). You have to show up for yourself. You are the employer and employee of your company (your dream). You must get this distinction. There is no one else to do it for you.

When you are hired for a job with a company, you cannot show up once in awhile and you cannot stop because someone said *no* to you. It must be the same with your dream, you must show up every day for that dream and you cannot stop.

So get on board and excited about you and your dream. It will be scary but so what! Do it anyway! Make your dreams come true no matter how big or small. You have examples of people all around you who made their dreams come true. You are no different. Why?

Girl, You're a Grown Ass Woman:, capable, strong, and worthy!

JUST FOR YOU!

In your journal, write out your dream in as much detail as possible.

Write out all the reasons or thoughts you have believed up until this poin which have kept you from your dream.

Look at the list above and turn each thought and reason into its opposite thus creating an affirmation for yourself.

Example:

Negative thought:

I'll never have the money to go into the recording studio.

Turn around thought:

I am a wonderful generator of money. I come up with ways to raise the money I need to go into the recording studio

Write about what is the worst that could happen if you go for your dream..............

The best that could happen.......

Continue.....

Take your dream(s) description from the pages above and turn it into one powerful and positive intention statement. This statement must stay in the present and begin with "I am."

Example: I am now an Interior Decorator running my own business and earning $4000 extra dollars per month.

Write a list of two or three tasks that you can do immediately that take you in the direction of your dream. Do this EVERYDAY until you achieve your dream. Give each item a deadline date.

When you hit a wall and can't move, be smart enough to call another GAW-friend!

CHAPTER 6

A GROWN ASS WOMAN IS A LIGHT IN THE WORLD

I realized after many years of playing victim in the world and having my ow
pity party day in and day out, that it was beginning to be boring. What
effect was I having in my life with an attitude of *I Can't* and *Poor Me?*
One that was not attractive, healthy, powerful, or bright.

I am a private music lessons teacher and the majority of my students are
girls between the ages of 9-18. I noticed that I would give them wise word
of advice about having a positive outlook in life and a positive outlook
about themselves in all aspects of their lives. After I awhile, I felt like a
fraud because I would hear myself say these amazing things to them and
realize that I wasn't even taking my own advice. We teach what we most
need to learn. **Our mess is our message to the world.**

I was asking them to implement behaviors of a Grown Ass Woman and I
wasn't being or doing what I advised them to be. For me, this had to
change. I have always been a champion for so many people in my life. It is
who I am by nature. But if I am saying the words but not living them mysel
it is inauthentic and dysfunctional. This was a big "aha moment" for me!

I had never used the phrase "Girl, You're a Grown Ass Woman!" until
two weeks before I started writing this book...Literally. It was a shock to
me when those words came out of my mouth. I had heard the phrase man
times before.

Yes, we are Grown Ass Women! I have now been saying these words everyday and all day long since, reminding myself "Girl, You're a Grown Ass Woman".

My life has changed. I am definitely walking my talk. I have become so aware of when I am not walking my talk. When I become fearful of anything or think I can't achieve something, I remind myself that I am a GAW and a GAW can achieve what she puts her mind to. A GAW knows that if she is not sure how to proceed or does not know something, she can find whatever she needs by asking an expert or looking it up and researching it. There is an answer to all we seek, but we must love ourselves enough to do and find what we need.

I no longer listen to the negativity that is going on in my mind. I bypass it. In the past, I would hook into the negativity and spiral down into sabotaging behaviors and thoughts until I was in a black hole. When you are in a black hole, there is no light and it seems you don't even know how to look for the light.

I feel now, I not only have a responsibility to myself to be a GAW but I have the responsibility to be that for all people that are in my world....small and globally. Being a light is infectious. When you stand up and claim the light that you are in all aspects of your life then you are showing those around you, young and old, male and female, black, white, brown, red that it is possible in their life as well.

If you have come from a family that from generation to generation did not recognize their light, guess what? They passed that on to you.

If you are reading this book, you now have the choice to change, to be different. When you have children, you get to pass it on to them. You car literally change the future generations of your entire family.

Life is all energy. We influence our environment with our energy. If you are in a funky, negative mood, those in your environment are influenced b, that energy. If you are positive, filled with life and happiness, then once again you are influencing your environment. People want positive and happy in their life. Trust me!

I know many of you came up in families that constantly downed you, affirmed your lousiness and worthlessness, and did nothing to prepare you for a bright future as a Grown Ass Woman, but your past does not define your future unless you allow it to. I am not saying anything new. YOU have the choice to change right now and at any given moment. YOU get to choose whether to be a light of power or a dark energy drain.

When we don't know our own power and our own Light then we become energy vampires. Energy vampires seek power from others by living out many sabotaging, dysfunctional actions toward themselves and others as well. These behaviors are very unconscious and it may take a few encounters with Light beings before we begin to notice how we are being

Even then, some may still say *no* to their own Light. I know, because I used to feel that I could not handle my own Light - that it would be too overwhelming. That in itself is a sabotaging thought and an excuse to not author our own life and a reason to stay in the dark.

There have been many GAWs before me and I always thought they were special type beings. My mother, my grand-mother, Maya Angelou, Oprah, Mother Teresa, Katherine Hepburn ...the list goes on. We think that to be real GAW, we have to do it in a big way. This is simply not the truth.

Choosing to be a GAW will change the quality of your life on every level. It is life affirming, life giving, and life nourishing. You can't help but influence others. They'll want to know what you've got, and who you are.

It is like the movie *It's a Wonderful Life!*. George Bailey didn't realize how many lives he had affected until his Guardian Angel showed him how life would have been had he not been born. In the movie, his whole town and his family are all affected negatively, all because he was never born. It is the same for all of us. We truly affect so many lives.

Becoming a GAW has caused me to have personal integrity, clearer boundaries, greater self-respect, greater self-esteem, be less altruistic, more loving, less fearful, and more confident. Becoming a GAW will cause others to become GAWs. Light attracts Light. Be a GAW for the sake of the world around you.

To know that I am that powerful with my actions and my words is life changing. I am not speaking of power in the sense that we as a society might think of power. Power to me is simply being centered in knowing who you are. I am not saying that everything in my life is perfect but I certainly don't feel disempowered.

I am not a girl anymore. I know that statement sounds so crazy in a sense, but so many women still live certain aspects of their lives with the mentality of a girl. This is so only because we were not taught how to be any different.

It is not for us to blame anyone, but it is important to know that we are all responsible for our own "growing up" once we've left home. For some, growing up happens earlier in life and for others it is later. No matter when it happens, celebrate it.

A friend of mine once said to me "You are either contributing to the world or contaminating the world." My interpretation of that statement is that you are either being a carrier of Light or a carrier of Darkness.

A GAW is a carrier of Light!

I am here to share with you that it feels so great to be on the path of contributing light instead of darkness. How about YOU?

JUST FOR YOU!

Name a couple of women in your life that you believe are GAWs and write about why you believe they are GAWs!

Write out a numbered list of one-line statements or words that describe their GAWness.

Example:

They don't take no for an answer.

Persistent

Write your own eulogy for your memorial service. What would you want people to say about you?

Translate your memorial into a numbered list of one-line statements or one-word qualities.

Print out the list and put it somewhere that is visible to you everyday!

Spend time meditating for five minutes a day. Sit comfortably in a chair cross-legged or on the floor. Begin by noticing your breath going in and going out. While breathing in, say to yourself *I am a Light.* And while breathing out, say to yourself *I am a Light!*

Breathing In - *I am a Light*

Breathing Out - *I am a Light*

Write about what impressions come up for you!

I know the word *meditation* scares a lot of people, but you are simply just sitting in a cross-legged position and watching your breath go in and out. The point is to allow all the thoughts of negativity to float by so that you can make way for that inner voice of clarity and knowing.

Go for a walk, and repeat "I am a Light" with every few steps. I am a Ligh

Many people walk to clear their minds or when they are blocked creatively or stuck. Walking shifts our energy.

As part of your daily ritual, say out loud "I am a Grown Ass Woman, I am Grown Ass Woman, I am a Grown Ass Woman!"

Make this statement a part of your day, all day. When you notice you are being fearful or feeling unworthy in any aspect of your life, remind yourself

am a GROWN ASS WOMAN:, capable, strong, and worthy!

CHAPTER 7

A GROWN ASS WOMAN KNOWS THERE IS A PRESENCE IN THE WORLD GREATER THAN HERSELF

I make this statement in such a way that it includes and does not exclude anyone's belief system. We all call this Presence something different. I can only hope that we are all tolerant enough to allow for this difference.

Some may call this presence God, or Allah, Buddha, Jesus, Jehovah, Holy Spirit, Spirit, The Great Spirit, Mother Nature. You get the idea.

A Grown Ass Woman knows that she does not walk in this world alone. There is a Presence that walks with her that is greater than she is. This Presence only seeks the best for her. Her relationship to this Presence is personal, divine, intimate and mysterious.

As a Grown Ass Woman, you must define this connection for yourself. Discover what this mystical Presence is for you. Begin a conversation between you and this Presence. You might start this conversation during a walk or during meditation. You might be by a river, the ocean, or a forest. And for some, it might be in a church, a mosque, a temple, an ashram, or a spiritual center. Go to whatever spot is sacred for you and begin this conversation. Ask questions and listen.

We are each like drops in the ocean. We are part of a greater whole. This greater whole, keeps the world going, keeps the rivers flowing, grass growing, snow falling, rain falling, blood flowing, hearts beating, etc.

So, do you see why you might want to connect with this greater whole?

Decide what you want this relationship to be. For me, I set my intentions and my goals before this Presence, whether that be about how to improve my finances or how I can forgive someone! It is up to you what you desire this relationship to look like.

During your meditation time is the best time to connect with this Presence.

Early mornings is the best time and late at night before you go to bed. Perhaps you might want to create a sacred space somewhere in your home that you go to everyday. Place any items or pictures that inspire you to feel the Divine. You might want to have affirmations, flowers, and candle.

Get connected and stay connected to this Presence. Starting your day out this way, will fuel how you interact in the world with others. And at night, you may take all that has happened during your day and offer it up and give thanks and gratitude for your life.

t is powerful as well as empowering to walk in the world with the
wareness of this Presence. A GAW knows this!

JUST FOR YOU!

Write about your belief in a Presence greater than you. What does that look like? What does it feel like?

you have not discovered this Presence in your life, simply ask this Presence to reveal itself during meditation. Try it. Write any observations you notice throughout your day.

Write a letter to this Presence regarding a particular problem or issue. Then respond back to yourself as if you were the Presence answering you back.

Example:

For me I would start out with.....

Dear God,

I am having a difficult time......

Then I would go to a blank page and write......

Dear Robin

It seems you might want to consider........

You will see this is a powerful tool. You will be surprised at your answers. Do this for anything that you need help with. The Presence speaks to us in many ways. Begin to practice being aware and awake. The more connected you are with the Presence, the more you will see synchronicities or "miracles" begin to appear more frequently!

Write about any experiences you have had in the past in which you were aware there was something greater at work, perhaps unexplainable.

CHAPTER 8

THE CHOICE

The Grown Ass Woman chooses to be a GAW. Her journey is one filled with many rewards inherent in it. Before hooking into the phrase, "Girl, you're a Grown Ass Woman," I didn't realize how much of an effec it would have on me. I formed a group on Facebook called GROWN ASS WOMEN UNITE! Within three days the group had over 30 women. Within those three days I wrote five chapters of this book and finished the book less than three weeks later.

In the past, I would have stopped all of these actions with thoughts of doubt and negativity, but this was bigger than me. Something greater took over and the site went up and the book was written. Once I decidec to be a Grown Ass Woman there was no going back.

I started to look at different aspects of my life, the first being my finance. My finances were a mess because I wasn't acting like a GAW. I had all kinds of excuses as to why my finances were out of control and the biggest excuse was that I was too overwhelmed to look at them or handle them. So I met with a financial coach to help me through the process of getting my financial behavior sober.

There were also relationships in my life that were messy because I was too fearful to be authentic and speak my truth to the situation and the persons involved. I realized that a GAW is not afraid to speak what's or her mind. So oddly enough I began speaking my truth.

did not even recognize myself. I spoke my truth in one particular situation and the other person thanked me for my honesty and we continue to work out our challenges.

After I ended my last relationship, I really took a hard look at what "girl" patterns I had played out. It was very difficult ending that relationship because he was truly a good man, but I was not the woman I wanted to be.

It was not ever the right relationship for me. I heard that voice at the beginning of the relationship and I ignored it.

We went full speed ahead. Crash and Burn.

Now as a GAW, I can take my time to listen and trust myself. I can take the time to listen to my potential partner. I can decide if the relationship is for me. I am capable and able to handle a Grown Up Relationship. Please understand that many people are in relationships or even married, but not as Grown Ass People. More than likely if neither person is Grown Ass, they are seeking for the other to fulfill them and make them happy. No one can do this for you! It is part of the reason we have such a high divorce rate. **Only two Grown Ass People can have a successful relationship or marriage.**

Since becoming a GAW, I have changed how I eat because I feel I am valuable enough and worthy enough to feel good in my own skin. I love clothes and I have been walking around in baggy clothes for the last 3 years eating what I've wanted and starting a diet and then stopping and then starting another and stopping and then another and another, etc..... know how to lose weight. It is a simple concept. Make healthier choices, move your body, and KNOW YOU ARE WORTH IT! A GAW doesn't fool herself with excuses upon excuses.

Another observation is I am now more organized. I take myself and my work seriously. I get to places on time. I follow through. I believe in the success of whatever I attempt. I have more energy, physically and mentall

These are just a few ways in which my life has changed since becoming aware of being a GAW. I know there is more to come. I am in my fifties and thinking about how great life is and not how it's all down hill from here or that it's too late. I know women who believe their life just happens to them and there is nothing they can do to affect change. You may not be able to control exactly what happens to you, but you can choose your response to what happens to you.

So the choice is up to you. In any given circumstance in your life you can choose to act like a GAW. Every woman knows what that looks like. I've had glimpses of my GAW since I was seven years old. It is not about that job you have, how much money you have, who you married...or didn't, but about how you feel about yourself!

JUST FOR YOU!

Create a list below beginning with the words:

I choose to (fill in the blank)

Example: I choose to be on time

I choose to follow through

I choose to..........

can only believe that this life was given to us to become the best and the most we can be. To move away from serving our ego to serving the greater whole. Serving the ego is what youngsters do because they know no different.

But at a certain point, we must all become aware of the difference.

WHEN I BECAME A WOMAN, I PUT AWAY CHILDISH THINGS

Put away childish patterns of behavior, ego driven behaviors, and instant gratification behaviors. Our walk in this life, I believe, is to walk toward the light, not into the darkness. Walk toward greater self-awareness, goodness, generosity, worthiness, love, joy, creativity, abundance, and wholeness.

Begin this journey from wherever you are right now in your life.

It is never too late. If you are living on this earth, you are a work in progress, not a finished product. We are always continuing to grow and unfold. Allow, Allow, Allow!

Don't forget to remind your friends, your mothers, your sisters, your daughters, your aunts and more importantly, yourself....

Girl, You're a Grown Ass Woman:, capable, strong, and worthy!

SOME GROWN ASS WOMEN PRINCIPLES!
(Add your own)

Grown Ass Women know their power.

Grown Ass Women think kindly of themselves.

Grown Ass Women follow their dreams to completion.

Grown Ass Women speak their minds.

Grown Ass Women are authentically themselves.

Grown Ass Women ask for clarification.

Grown Ass Women do not guess what other people are thinking.

Grown Ass Women allow space and time for inner quiet .

Grown Ass Women know what they want.

Grown Ass Women speak aloud what they desire and intend.

Grown Ass Women are not afraid of anger, theirs or others.

Grown Ass Women call another Grown Ass Woman for advice if needed.

Grown Ass Women when dating contemplate whether the love interest has the qualities they desire instead of wondering if the love interest desires them.

Grown Ass Women will never allow a love interest to come between her and a friend.

Grown Ass Women surround themselves with beauty.

Grown Ass Women pamper themselves like queens.

Grown Ass Women speak their truth gently and firmly.

Grown Ass Women know they are a Light in the world.

Grown Ass Women know there is enough in the world.

Grown Ass Women do not believe in lack.

Grown Ass Women handle their finances with finesse.

Grown Ass Women keep their word.

Grown Ass Women *intend* their lives instead of living by default.

Grown Ass Women are consistent and persistent.

Grown Ass Women do not give up.

WORDS TO KNOW

GAW   Grown Ass Woman

GAW-licious A delicious Grown Ass Woman

GAW-geous A gorgeous Grown Ass Woman

GAW-dly   A Godly Grown Ass Woman

GAW-friend(s)   Grown Ass Women friends

GAW-ness   Awareness of being a Grown Ass Woman

GAW-dess   A Grown Ass Woman with qualities of a Goddess

34322721R00060

Made in the USA
San Bernardino, CA
26 May 2016